Southern Sounds

by Susan Ring

HOUGHTON MIFFLIN   BOSTON

It stirs up feelings. It tells stories. It makes you want to stomp your feet and sing along.

Southern music isn't just one sound. It ranges from slow, story-telling blues to upbeat Cajun, from Dixieland horns to the washboard strums of Zydeco. Read about this cornerstone of American music and the musicians who have made it come alive.

Jazz

In New Orleans, Louisiana, in the late 1800s, a new kind of music took root — jazz. It grew out of many other types of music, including African folk songs, Caribbean music, and the blues.

Strange to say, it was partly through funerals that jazz was born. Funeral parades were common in New Orleans at the turn of the 20th century. Brass bands marched through the streets playing trumpets, trombones, and clarinets. But this band music was deeper and more personal than usual parade music.

Around 1890, two new styles of music came to New Orleans. One style was called ragtime. It set old songs to new, playful rhythms. Ragtime was played mainly on the piano. For the next 25 years, it was the most popular form of music in America.

A music style called the *blues* also became popular at that time. It grew out of many Southern locations, such as the Mississippi River delta. It was deeply emotional and often used a style of call and response. That was the way people sang in church. The words in a blues song told a story.

All of these styles — marching band, ragtime, blues, and other local sounds — contributed to early jazz.

In 1917, the Original Dixieland Jazz Band made the first recording of jazz. *Dixieland* was a common nickname for the Southern states. But the Original Dixieland Jazz Band was

The Original Dixieland Jazz Band, 1917

actually formed in Chicago. It wasn't long before the sound of "Dixieland jazz" became popular all around the country.

Jazz changed over the years. Musicians added their own styles. If you listened to many of them play, you might never hear the same music twice. Maybe the reason lies deep in African American history.

During the 1800s, thousands of enslaved people came to the South from Africa and the West Indies. Along with the pain of slavery, they faced strange new languages and cultures. One of the ways they survived was to *improvise*. This means that in their everyday life they had to be creative, make do with what they found, and make things up as they went along.

Jazz reflects all of this: the emotion, the variety, and the creativity. A big part of jazz is improvising. Musicians begin playing the notes that are written down. Then they play something of their own, making it up as they go along. Musicians take turns talking to each other, not with words, but with notes. It is like a conversation using instruments.

Jazz is music of freedom. It's a way for a group to come together as a band, but each person in the band can express his or her own sound.

"Jazz washes away the dust of everyday life."

— Art Blakey, jazz drummer

Louis Armstrong

Louis Armstrong was born in New Orleans in 1901. He grew up in a rough section known as the "Battlefield." At age twelve, he went to reform school. It was there that he taught himself the cornet, a smaller version of the trumpet. From 1917 through 1919, he played in New Orleans and St. Louis, Missouri. More and more people began to talk about the music of Louis Armstrong.

In the 1920s, Armstrong moved to Chicago to join the popular band of "King" Oliver. Then he went out on his own. He formed bands called the Hot Five and the Hot Seven. He made recordings. When people heard Armstrong's records they were amazed at his warm yet powerful trumpet playing.

Armstrong's bands played all around the world. People loved to hear his trumpet solos. Many felt that he could improvise like no one else. They also loved his warm personality. Once Armstrong was asked what he thought good music was. He answered, "Anything you pat your foot to is good music."

Scat Singing

Ella Fitzgerald was a famous jazz singer. She used her voice like a jazz instrument. In her singing, she sometimes used nonsense words and phrases. But these phrases had a lot of rhythm and feeling. This type of singing is called *scat singing*. Legend has it that Louis Armstrong invented scat singing when he forgot the lyrics of a song in 1926. While the legend probably isn't true, Armstrong, Ella Fitzgerald, and other singers helped make scat a popular jazz tool.

Ella Fitzgerald

Cajun Music

Cajun music grew out of the American South but it was sung in French. Its name tells where it came from, a place thousands of miles to the north. *Cajun* is a short way of saying *Acadian*, or "from Acadia."

Acadia was part of the Canadian province of Nova Scotia in the 1700s. At that time, Britain ruled Nova Scotia. The Acadians, however, were French-speaking and refused to be loyal to the British king and queen. The British forced them to leave.

Many Acadians ended up in the southwestern part of Louisiana. It was here in the late 19th century that Cajun music began. The Acadians brought with them their old French folk songs. Their songs reflected their sad feelings of having to leave home.

They formed bands using the fiddle, accordion, and triangle. Many people made their own instruments and passed stories down to their children through their songs. Over time, Acadians became known as Cajuns.

The Cajun Sound

The fiddle, or violin, joins the accordion in most Cajun music. Today you might also hear drums and banjo. You can also hear people sing Cajun songs without using any instruments at all.

Cajun band

The Cajuns take great pride in their land and heritage. Their music reflects these feelings. In Louisiana, the Acadians lived among a variety of other cultures. Some of their neighbors were people from the Caribbean and West Indies, other Europeans, and Native Americans. The Cajuns heard blues, country music, and other types of popular music. They put these sounds into their music. You can hear bits and pieces of all of these in the Cajun sound.

Zydeco

Creole music grew up in Louisiana along with Cajun music. It was started by African Americans who spoke French. Like Cajun music, Creole music uses the guitar, fiddle, triangle, and accordion.

In the late 1940s, Creole musicians began to hear jazz and blues on the radio and in dance halls. They added these sounds to their music. Then they stopped playing the fiddle and added a new rhythm instrument, the washboard. This became a new form of music called Zydeco (ZY-duh-ko).

The word *zydeco* probably comes from *les haricots*, the French words for beans. "The beans aren't salty," was a common Creole expression for hard times, when salted meat was scarce.

Zydeco is a mixture of jazz, blues, rock, and French music. While you will seldom hear a fiddle in a Zydeco band, you will usually hear an accordion, a triangle, a guitar, and a washboard.

Most likely the washboard players will be wearing thimbles on their fingers. That makes the strumming easier. In more recent years, Zydeco bands have added a saxophone or other horns to the sound. Today, Zydeco songs are in English and even have elements of hip-hop.

A Zydeco musician playing a washboard

Clifton Chenier

For more then thirty years, a man named Clifton Chenier (sheh-NEER) was a popular Zydeco musician. Many people call him the "King of Zydeco." Early in his career, Chenier played his music in church. As he traveled around to play concerts, more and more people got to know him. He made Creole people feel proud of their music. In the 1980s, Chenier won an accordion contest in Europe. It was here that he was crowned "King of Zydeco." He won a Grammy Award in 1984. Clifton Chenier died in 1987, but his son C.J. still plays his music. His band is called "The Red Hot Louisiana Band."

Clifton Chenier at the New Orleans Jazz Festival, 1983

Country Music

Northeast of Louisiana, in the Appalachian Mountains, people played their fiddles and sang in a style called *old time music*. This was the music of square dancing. The musicians mostly used stringed instruments — banjo, fiddle, and guitar. They worked regular jobs. They were miners, farmers, carpenters, and preachers. They played at house parties and church events. But few were able to leave their jobs and become full-time musicians.

Old time music was based on music of the English and Scots-Irish people who had settled in the South. Later on, the blues spread from New Orleans up the Mississippi River, and added its soulful quality to old-time music. In the 1920s, country music became popular around the nation.

Today, country music has many different sounds. You can hear slow country ballads. You can hear fast, happy, foot-stomping songs. The main instrument in country music is the guitar.

In the 1940s, people made new changes in country music. They called it country and western music. It used cowboy themes and reflected a western way of life. Songs included more lonesome, sad, topics.

Grand Ole Opry

Nashville, Tennessee, is a city known for its country music. Many singers and musicians got their start there and work there today. One place in Nashville has seen just about all of them. It's the stage of a radio program called the "Grand Ole Opry." Since 1925, when it was called "The WSM Barn Dance," the Grand Ole Opry has played host to the top country performers in the U.S, from Bill Monroe to Loretta Lynn. These concerts were part of a radio show on Saturday nights. People around the country would sit in front of their radios and listen to country music. Today it remains the world's longest-running live radio program. Every year people travel from all over the United States to hear concerts there.

Bluegrass band on stage at the Grand Ole Opry

The Little Lute

The mandolin is a small version of an old Italian instrument, the mandola, or lute. One popular type of mandolin has four pairs of steel strings and an oval-shaped hole in the middle. In the early 1900s, people started forming mandolin orchestras. They played all different sizes of mandolins, creating both high and low sounds. The style of mandolin played in bluegrass music has a special flat back.

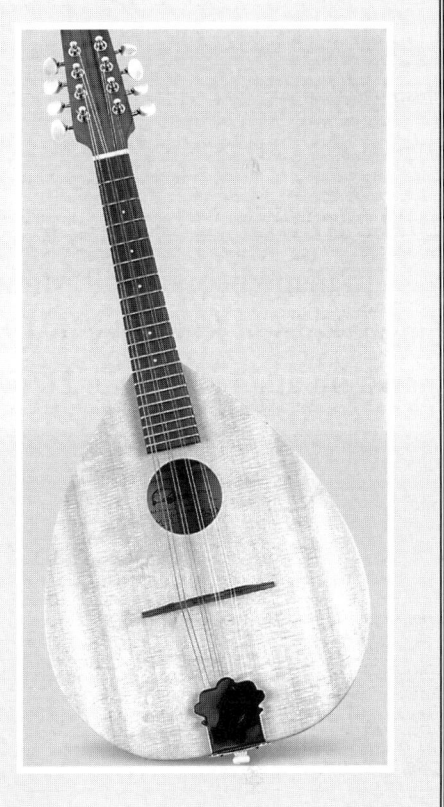

Bluegrass

Bluegrass is named for the "Bluegrass state" of Kentucky, where it was born. The tempo is usually quick and full of energy. You could take almost any type of song and play it in a bluegrass style. Bluegrass is string-band music. So you will most likely hear such string instruments as banjo, fiddle, mandolin, and guitar in a bluegrass band. You might also hear harmonica. However, you won't hear electric guitar or drums in traditional bluegrass music! A bluegrass song might have singers, as well. They will often sing in high harmonies that come from church gospel hymns.

Bill Monroe

To many people, Bill Monroe is the father of bluegrass music. Born in Kentucky in 1911, Bill taught himself the mandolin at an early age. He wanted to play the fiddle or

guitar, but both his brothers already played those instruments. So at age ten, he picked up the mandolin and taught himself how to play. As he got better at the mandolin, his brother Charlie let him try his guitar. In a short time, Bill was playing the guitar in public. People loved his music.

Bill Monroe

Bill got to know a popular guitar player named Arnold Schultz. Schultz was an African American musician. He drew large crowds whenever he played in concert. Bill was just a young teenager when Schultz asked Bill to play with him at a dance. They were still playing music when the sun rose the next morning.

Bill's father died when Bill was only sixteen. At that time, he went to live with his brothers in Indiana. During the week, the brothers cleaned out oil barrels for an oil company. On the weekends, Bill played his mandolin while his brothers played fiddle and guitar. Two years later, Bill was playing music full time. He and his brother, Charlie, became the Monroe Brothers.

Bill later became formed a group called the Blue Grass Boys. His group changed the way country string bands played music. Bill based his music on the old fiddle bands he used to hear in the South. But he introduced new harmonies and rhythms that had never been heard played by a traditional string band. Bill also had players step forward and play a solo. He sang in a style that was called *high lonesome singing*. He also added church harmonies and faster tempos. He even dressed differently. Bill's band performed wearing white shirts, boots and cowboy hats.

The Del McCoury Band playing bluegrass in Nashville, Tennessee, 1996

By the 1950s, more and more people began playing Bill's style of music. In 1970, he was elected into the Country Music Hall of Fame. Bill Monroe began a new style of music and paved the way for all other bluegrass musicians who came after him.

Southern music is a good example of how music picks up the styles and ideas that came before it. Whether it is bluegrass, jazz, or Zydeco, Southern musicians have borrowed ideas from the culture around them, then made the music their own.